The Table With No Edge

Lucy Sheffield

The Table with No Edge

To,

Gorgeous Claire,

Always follow your heart, Always do whats right for you.

love your life, have fun.

Always remember how amazing + unique you are.

Dare 2 Bu Claire, Enjoy the book!

loads of big lesbo love

Lulu Belle
xxx
xx

Lucy Sheffield

Text copyright © 2018 Lucy Sheffield All Rights Reserved

ISBN: 97819769673766

All rights reserved. No part of this publication may be reproduced, stored in or introduced into a retrieval system, or transmitted, in any form, or any means (electronic, mechanical, photocopying, recording or otherwise) without the prior written permission of the author or publisher.

The Table with No Edge

Lucy Sheffield

Acknowledgements

I want to say a special thanks to Debra Simmons, who very kindly gave me a lot of her time (and still does) in helping me to understand the nature of thought & the principles.

I am eternally grateful for learning this, its mind-blowing stuff and as she often says it's all about staying in the conversation, hearing things over and over again gaining new insights daily.

It is most certainly life changing. I cannot put into words how wonderful my life now is, and how much fun we all have.

For more information Debra can be contacted through her website
www.debrasimmons.co.uk.

Also, thanks so much to Julie Weeks and Beccy Sheffield in helping me with the editing of this book... you guys are super amazing. They are both a part of Debra's company Dare2BU and can also be contacted through the above website.

Lucy Sheffield

Dedication

I would love to dedicate this book to
Janine Leaf.
A good friend of mine who sadly passed
away in July 2017.
When this happened I was very much
inspired to continue creating my book,
follow my passion of living in Devon, doing
what I love – sharing the principles & helping
others to live a life that they love.

Lucy Sheffield

Table of Contents

Acknowledgements 4
Dedication 6
Table of Contents 7
Introduction 12

Chapter 1: Innocently Thinking 14

Chapter 2 - A Shaken up Snow Globe Versus A Quiet Mind 24

Chapter 3 - What Are the 3 Principles 29

Chapter 4 - Story Time 42

Chapter 5 - Loving yourself Unconditionally 47

Chapter 6 - Letting go for a Peaceful Feeling 56

Chapter 7 - We Are All the Same 63

Chapter 8 – Fun 72

Chapter 9 - Life is an Illusion 79

Chapter 10 - Bye Bye for Now 88

About the Author 90

The Table with No Edge

Lucy Sheffield

The Table With No Edge

The Table with No Edge

Lucy Sheffield

Introduction

If a table has no edges, then where does it begin or end?
In this book we are going to help you see, to put it simply, it doesn't!

We are also going to explore the similarities between the unlimited human potential, which we all have access to and the edgeless table.

By the end of this book you will, hopefully, have a deeper understanding of what we, as human beings, have been missing and you will begin to discover why the table has no edges.

Throughout this book the most important thing I want you to do is have fun reading it! Life to me is like a game of monopoly; we are the players doing the best we can to enjoy the game and learn from our mistakes, but we aren't in control, not by a long shot!

Will we win, or will we lose? Who knows, who cares? But let's play and have some fun along the way...

Lucy Sheffield

Chapter 1 – Innocently Thinking

Would it blow your world apart, if I were to tell you everything you think is all made up? Or would you agree?

Before I began my personal journey to a better quality of life, I thought everything I knew was true. I mean, it must be, right? Why would we even have thinking if it wasn't serving a purpose?

OK, before I begin to blow your world apart, and probably your mind, I would like you to think for a few minutes about everything you think you already know about how life works.

Now forget it all - yeah, I mean ALL, because what you are about to discover is the truth, and boy is it GOOOOOD...

Ready?

Then let's begin!

Lucy Sheffield

I reckon you would agree that most of us spend our lives searching for happiness (I will take that as a yes). And most of us don't end up getting it, because when things happen that we didn't want, or ask for, it looks like it has caused us upset, dragging us down and down on that spiral into despair. And once we are down how difficult does it look to get back up again? Almost impossible, right?

Well, for most of us we are innocently looking for happiness in the wrong place; outside of our own selves.
As I'm sure you have heard many times by the wise people in this world, look inside, you will find what you are after. Well guess what? They are right.
From the moment we are born we are given everything we ever need to equip us in this life.

Sound simple?

Yeah you are right, it is.

Yep I hear your argument loud and clear... Well it sure doesn't look that way to me! Ask yourself this question, does everything look to you the way it actually is?

There are a lot of things in life that look a certain way, but it doesn't necessarily mean they are, or that they work that way. An example of this could be a straw put into a glass of water (go on, go try it, I know you want to). So, the straw- when it hits the water - looks bent. Is the straw really bent? No, it is an illusion (in case you were stuck). It only appears to be bent, but we know the straw hasn't changed at all, it is still in the same form it was before it went into the water.

I'm sure, by now, you are thinking "what on earth has this got to do with my innocent thinking?", well I promise you I am getting to that!

OK, so what we tend to miss in life is that every human being on planet earth is innocently believing their thinking.

100% of the time. It is only our thinking that gets in the way of our innate peacefulness. It sure as hell looks like it's the neighbour annoying us, or the boss picking on us, or our other half being lazy. But what we miss is that they have nothing to do with it. For us to experience any feeling about anything, yes ANYTHING, it must pass via our own thought system.

I'm afraid to tell you that YOU are the only one responsible for your feelings. It is never anything outside of you causing you to feel a certain way, EVER! Feelings can only come from within. Nobody can put a feeling into our heads.

As I said before, there are so many times in our lives when it doesn't look that way, but I can promise you, you will never find anything outside of you to cause you a feeling. Be it happy or sad, good or bad, it always comes from YOU.

For example, imagine when you are in a bad mood, your partner may do something that looks like it has really upset you. However, the next day they do the same thing, but because you are in a better mood it looks totally different to you. So, the way you experience it changes, and it has absolutely nothing to do with that person and everything to do with YOU.

Every single one of us here on earth experiences things differently. We see the world and the people in it through our eyes and our eyes only. However, despite our different outlooks we are all made of the same stuff, underneath the thinking. We are all on a journey; seeking happiness. (I suppose the odd few would argue). Whether we make it or not purely depends on our quality of thinking, which changes moment to moment.

Once we begin to understand how our thinking affects us, we naturally begin to change, viewing the world and everyone in it from a totally different level than we have ever seen before. And I can tell you from personal experience it looks absolutely fabulous from up here!

Lucy Sheffield

I'm going to give you another example of how our thinking works.

Imagine a glass lift.

Now imagine you are in the lift, going up and down the levels. On each floor there is something new and different to see. More than likely when you are in the basement you won't be able to see much at all, and when you rise up to the first floor you will see a little more, as the view becomes clearer. The further up the floors you go, the more you can see, the clearer you can see, and once at the top, WOW the view is just so amazing that you don't really want to go back down to the basement too often. I mean, why would you when you can see such a beautiful view from up here?

So now I want you to spend the day going up and down the lift at your local shopping centre (joke)

Well, effectively, this is exactly the same way the mind works, moment to moment. Our thinking goes up and down all-day long. Imagine, if you will, the basement being likened to our sad, angry or depressive thinking. Then as you rise up to the first floor, your thinking is slightly clearer, you aren't feeling sad, angry, or having depressive thoughts. They are more likely to be nicer, happier, joyful thoughts, and by the time you reach the top floor your thinking is just lovely and amazing. Everything that looked so horrible from the basement view, now looks so gorgeous you feel like singing and dancing with joy.

For most of us we have no idea that this is what is actually going on all the time. We innocently think there is something wrong with us if we are feeling sad, angry, or depressed, when realistically we are only feel our thinking in that moment. AND the good news is that our thinking changes, without us having to do anything.

It is how our system, which allows us to experience life, is set up to work. Exactly the same as a wound – it will heal if left alone. It is self-correcting. This system only fails when we interfere, innocently thinking we know best and we need to do something to "sort ourselves out" or "fix what is broken". There is nothing broken though. It is just our thinking doing its thing. And the more we begin to see this, the less power we give to our thoughts, allowing them to just pass through us. Again, as with the straw in the water, it really doesn't look like it works this way, but it does!

Simples!

The very nature of thought is to assist in guiding us through life, but we don't need it to be our master. It is designed to act as a servant, helping where we need it, but not hindering us when we don't. When thought is your master, you will not find the happiness within you. However, when your understanding of the nature of thought deepens, thought will serve you as intended, and from this place, happiness will begin to radiate from deep within your soul.

So now we have touched upon the nature of thought, in the next chapter, we are going to explore some more into how it affects us when our mind has too many thoughts racing around it.

Night night... sleep well, pick me up again tomorrow for more fun, fun, fun and learning in chapter 2!

Lucy Sheffield

Chapter 2 – A Shaken Up Snow Globe Versus a Quiet Mind

Good morning, afternoon or evening....

Hopefully you are following so far, and I hope you enjoyed chapter 1. If so, you are really going like chapter 2!

We were only warming up in the first chapter. In this chapter we are going to get boiling hot. I have loads and loads more metaphors for you - the best ones. These are really going to help you to understand where your experience is coming from. Firstly, I'd like to touch upon how the mind works better with less on it. As I'm sure many of you have heard before, we work so much more productively with less on our minds. I mean, it's pretty obvious really when we think about it. There must be times you can recall, in your life so far, when you have literally done things without having to think about it.

For example, when we sit down, we don't start saying to ourselves "oh right, ok then, now let me just turn around, bend my knees in the right way and fall back onto the cushion" do we?
How daft does that sound?
So, what do we do? We just "do it" without trying. And the results tell the story for themselves (apart from those of you who always miss and end up on the floor, but that's a whole other story).

So, what I'm pointing to here is that when we have less on our minds and we are just in the flow of life, everything is less of an effort. I'm guessing that now, what you want to know is, "what technique do I need then to have less on my mind?" or "how do I do it?" Well, sorry to tell you this but I don't have those kinds of answers for you. As I said in chapter 1, you have all the answers inside you already.

There is nothing for us to do.

But for your thinking, you are innately happy. Your happiness can become clouded over with the thinking you have taken as true. We are born happy, we just forget we are!

The Table with No Edge

As suggested in the chapter title, our thoughts can be likened to a snow globe.

Shake it up and what do you get?

Well the nice picture in the background (our awareness or innate happiness) is still there, we just can't see it very clearly, due to all the snow (thinking).

So, what do we do with the snow globe? Do we interrupt it? Does it need help? Or will it settle down on its own if we leave it alone? I reckon, you are clever enough to know the answer to this one!

Yipeeee!

You got it right, we don't need to do anything, the snow will settle on its own. When it does the nice picture in the background will be visible once again, because that's what snow globes do. Exactly the same as what our mind does.

Lucy Sheffield

As human beings, we miss this simple trick of thought. The link that we miss is that our feelings are created by our thoughts, but of course thought is invisible. We cannot see it, so therefore, we simply forget that it exists; although it is always running the show from behind the scenes.

Just like the snow globe, when our thinking settles down, we have a clear mind and can see the bigger picture, which is always there in the background but clouded with our thinking.

The clear picture is what we are looking for in life, a clear mind. Within this space there is room for new, fresh thinking. The quiet mind is where miracles happen. Once we begin to understand this, we start to go to our quiet mind more often, leaving behind the shaken-up snow globe.

The Table with No Edge

Chapter 3 - What Are The 3 Principles?

Wow, chapter 3 already and you are still reading, give yourself a pat on the back!

Seriously though, I hope you are enjoying it so far, after all life is for having fun and that's what we want to achieve by the end of this book, if nothing else...

In this chapter I want to go back a few years to your childhood (I can appreciate this is a long time for some of you he he). OK, so if you don't want to go there, then please think of a child you know right now, maybe around the age of 2/3 years old.
They are just getting to the stage of discovering how to walk/talk etc. and most of the time they are into anything they can get their hands on in that moment. If you will, spend a little time watching them, and see if you notice what I have...

Children, to me, seem innocent - they are not yet affected by their experiences. What I mean by this is, if you watch a 2-year-old fall over and hurt themselves, they may cry or scream for a few minutes wanting love and hugs from you, but it passes very quickly. Time how long this lasts, because it normally isn't very long at all, within a few minutes they have forgotten all about it and suddenly want the ice cream they can see their older sister is eating. My point here is, children don't hold on to any thoughts/feelings for very long, because it doesn't make sense to them to do so. They live moment to moment without a care in the world. No worries, stress, anxiety.
They don't buy into all of that.
And notice how peaceful children are.

Well, to me it looks like they are the most peaceful, happiest little souls on this planet. It looks to me like we can learn a hell of a lot from these little people. They haven't lost sight of their happiness, it isn't covered up by dodgy thinking.

This is the 3 principles in action.

Lucy Sheffield

From the moment we are born, to the moment we die, we live in the feeling of our thinking.

That's it, NOTHING more.

Unfortunately, as we get older, it doesn't look like it can be that simple. We complicate it by finding another explanation of why we feel the way we do. We strive to find happiness from elsewhere, missing the easiest, simplest trick of the mind, that in fact, we only need to look inside. We only need to understand where our experience is coming from – thought in the moment, and it's only ever temporary.

We have everything we ever need within us. Yeah sure, it can look as though it would help if we had a little more money and people were kinder, or we can drive a flash car. But let me tell you some of the happiest people I know have no material things at all, but they do have very little clouding their minds.

Take a look at some actors/actresses or famous people. Some of them we see in the media are constantly taking drugs, drinking themselves to death - does that look like happiness to you? Because it sure doesn't look like my definition of the word. (I'm going off on one now aren't I – sorry!)

But my point is, money, fame, nice cars etc. etc., sure do look like they make you happy, but it simply isn't true, or it only lasts momentarily. It isn't a constant feeling. It only lasts until the next fix.

Take a look at the poor children in the third world countries where there is a lack of water/food etc. If you look closely you will see even though they have hardly anything material, they are happy.

Why? Because they haven't had anything else. They don't constantly feel the need to have anything else. They really appreciate the little they do have; it means so much to them.

I've also noticed how people with very little always share what they have as well. It blows my mind, because it looks to me like, "hello you have hardly anything, yet you are willing to share it".

The 3 principles (Mind, Thought and Consciousness) points us in the direction of happiness, or peace from within. They are the system behind the human experience. The foundations from where we create our realities. They are a constant, never changing....

"they are the basic building blocks, and it is through these 3 components that all psychological mysteries are unfolded"

Sydney Banks

The 3 principles were uncovered by a guy named Sydney Banks around 40 years ago. He was a regular Scottish guy, a welder by trade, who had what he described as a life changing epiphany.

I'm not 100% sure what happened but the story goes something like this... he was at a meeting and was talking to a friend or co-worker about feeling insecure, and this chap pointed out to him that he wasn't insecure at all, he just thought he was. Syd seemed to see this so deeply & insightfully that it changed him mentally & even physically, and he made it his life's work to spread the word of what he had seen, and how it could change the world as we know it. You can find out more about Sydney Banks by googling him.

The 3 principles are pointing to the truth. The truth inside us all, that we have forgotten about. Forgotten that we are these amazing, unique spiritual beings enjoying our human life experiences, which we innocently create via the power of thought. All too easily we have covered this truth over with our negative thinking, hence blaming others for our feelings.

Mind, Thought and Consciousness work together behind the scenes, creating our experience of life. My personal favourite metaphor, to explain how they work together, is likening them to an old cinema projector (it's a lot easier to draw this out, but I will do my best to try explaining) ...

Mind - The intelligence behind all things in life, or as I like to say the main source of connection or the power source (if I was drawing it, it would be a plug socket where I would plug in the projector)

Thought – The power to create our reality moment to moment, and for the purpose of the drawing, thought comes into play as the old film reel. So again, try to imagine reels and reels of film, each one producing a different scene, i.e. a horror film, a romantic film, a comedy etc. etc.

Consciousness – Our thoughts brought to life. Consciousness is like the light that shines on the film reel and projects the image onto the screen bringing the film to life, whether that be a horror, romance or comedy.

I hope you are following me so far, because once we grasp this on a deep level, through insight, and not intellect, then this is when we will begin to notice a change in our quality of thinking. The by-product of the insight is a new quality, or lease, of life.

I will continue to explain how I see this as insightful learning, rather than learning through intellect.

When we are at school, learning how to add up and learning new words etc., we are learning through techniques that somebody else has found helpful. We are therefore copying somebody else's ideas (thoughts) and are doing this through our brain, trying to make sense of it.

Insightful learning is more about being in the feeling, there is nothing to make sense of because it is already a part of who we are. It literally means a ***"sight from within"***.

It is more of a personal thing to each of us, because we are all unique and have our own way of seeing things.

As Sydney Banks always used to say,

"don't listen to the words, look behind them for a feeling,"

He also said when listening to the principles, listen as if you are listening to music, don't try to figure anything out, or work out what you think it all means.

As human beings we tend to want to try and work something out, we think we need to be doing something to get somewhere. Whereas, in fact, the easiest way to begin a transformation through this simple understanding is to do nothing, just relax, let the words sink in and continue with your life.

You will notice, gradually for some people, and overnight for others (as I said we are all different and unique), things will begin to change for you.

The strangest thing is, nothing in the outside world will be different but inside (where it counts and all stems from) EVERYTHING will feel different. You may start to notice that you feel calmer about things that once used to bug you (you may not as well).

When we truly begin to see how our experience is being created behind the scenes, it's like a weight being lifted off your mind. A sense of freedom kicks in and we begin to realise it's all created in the moment.

If we have created it then we can re-create whatever we like, any time we like. I mean OMG isn't that just soooo amazingly wonderful, powerful and incredibly liberating?

We are literally artists with a blank canvas. Every new thought we have is like a new splash of paint on the blank canvas, creating a new exciting part of our picture.

What would you prefer to be creating on your canvas?

Colourful, happy, vibrant pictures or dull, lifeless, boring pictures. The choice really is yours!

So, to sum up, the principles point to the fact that we live in the feeling of our thinking 100% of the time.

Nothing, or anyone, outside of us, can give us a feeling, or make us feel a certain way.

For example, your partner's behaviour doesn't annoy you, it's how you are thinking about them in that moment that makes you feel annoyed.

Simple isn't it? Yet so profound!

So, what are you waiting for, get creating!! Come on, I give you until chapter 5 to re-create something new, then I want to see these wonderful creations...

Sleep well my lovely new friend...

Lucy Sheffield

Chapter 4 – Story Time

Full Steam ahead now! Chapter 4 already, amazing!

I don't know about you, but I am really enjoying myself. In this chapter I would like to attempt to explain to you how we make everything up and don't even realise it. I think the easiest way to see how this is happening, is to first watch/listen to somebody else doing it, i.e. creating their stories.

You will notice it everywhere.

The hardest part is recognising that you are also doing it.

Again, it sure doesn't look like you are, because our own personal stuff looks very real and true to us. But it isn't. I find I tended to be able to justify my stories with a "yeah but" ….

Now, when I hear myself saying "yeah but…" it indicates to me that it looks like something other than thought has created my experience.

If every single thing we experience is coming to us via our thinking in the moment - and thinking changes - then how can anything (yes absolutely ANYTHING) be more than a story we have made up?

Question everything, be open, and see what comes up for you. You will be amazed, the stuff you thought had no other way of being anything else will fall away. And once that falls away, there are new stories to be created. So much fun to be had!

There is always another way to see things, a fresh thought giving you a whole new perspective on things, waiting around the corner. And boy does it get better and better the deeper you look in this direction. The more you can open up to the possibility that NOTHING is set in stone, the more things will shift, creating you the nicest experiences in life.

You know that floaty feeling in your tummy you might sometimes experience when you feel happy, well I can assure you that is constantly available, and you feel it more often when you are open to things being a different way.

It is only when we are stuck in a dark place, believing the stories we have made up, taking them to be the God's honest truth that we don't feel so good.

We cannot see there is possibly another way this can be viewed, as we can only see things from where we are standing.

As human beings we like to try and analyse everything, always believing there is an explanation for things; over complicating things. If this were a school subject, I'm sure we would all get A*.

How often do you find yourself saying "oh I bet he/she thinks I'm an idiot for doing x/y/z"

Be honest now!

We constantly think we know what someone else is thinking, and we base that on how we may think that ourselves, if we were in that situation. After all that is the only tool we have available to use.

So, keep remembering it is only another story you have made up and you will go far. The more you continue to look in that direction, the more you will see.

The Table with No Edge

Chapter 5 – Loving yourself unconditionally

So, you may be thinking chapter 4 was small? Yeah that is because I don't have many stories to tell any more lol.

OK now this chapter is about to get deep! You are going to love it... It is the beginning of the new you.

We are going to look at loving ourselves, for this is where we need to begin in order to have a wonderful life. We need the foundations in place, to build on.

I believe that for many of us we think we love ourselves, but when we really look at this deeply we begin to see actually we don't!

I would say a lot of people see it as a selfish act, but once we can see that we are all waves in the same ocean, then why wouldn't you love and respect yourself.

Like with the ocean we are one large sea of energy. We are all connected as humans, yet the power of thought gives us the illusion of separation, just like the waves in the ocean. It appears that there are separate waves, but it is all just one body of water.

When we can really see our true human potential, there is no way you wouldn't love yourself.

I mean, what is there not to love?

Human beings are amazing creatures. Often, the things we take for granted are actually amazing achievements. For example, making aeroplanes that carry people through the sky to another part of the world… if that isn't just the cleverest invention I don't know what is!

People have been able to produce such amazing things because of their knowledge of the principle of gravity. Understanding the principles of how life works enables us to live fuller lives.

It looks very apparent to me that in order to love somebody else, we need to know how to do that and what better way than learning to love ourselves first.

One of my favourite phrases is "you cannot give to somebody else what you do not have" how true is that?

It just is not possible!

Our state of mind changes moment to moment (as we have discussed) which means we are constantly thinking different things. If our state of mind is low, we are likely to have low thoughts about ourselves, maybe believing we are stupid or horrible.

However, when our state of mind then shoots up a level or 2 (remember the glass lift) then our thoughts are of a better quality. We begin to think we are nice, kind people. Simply understanding this can help our state of mind to be higher more of the time. We learn not to listen to the negative thoughts as we realise we are just 'in the basement' and we don't need to trust our thinking from this low level.

So, understanding this deeper and deeper results in us beginning to love ourselves. And as a result of loving ourselves we can love others more easily, because we understand how to do it.

We can show others how to do it too, for example, all you need to do is constantly give the best you have to offer without expecting anything in return. That even includes a 'Thank you'.

We don't need another person to thank us for something we have done if we are truly giving without wanting anything back. For someone to thank you is a reflection of them. (and I'm sure there are plenty of times you have forgotten to thank someone for something without realising it, it never means we are a bad person, we just didn't have that pass through our thought system at that time).

Isn't it always really nice to be nice. A lot of the time we have trouble doing this because we want people to show gratitude. However, the more we give unconditionally, the more we get.

It's the flow of life.

But even if we don't get anything back, it is just a nice feeling for ourselves to keep giving, unconditionally. Often, we beat ourselves up for doing "wrong/bad" things when all we need to do is realise that we are human, and we make mistakes. We simply need to forgive ourselves and move on.
If we forgive ourselves, again we are teaching others to forgive us too.

We can learn from our mistakes, helping us play the game of life in a much better way. Think about the people in your life and how you think they see you...

Do you think they view you as worthy of loving?

It's another illusion of course, but it does look like other people are nice and kind and more beautiful than ourselves. It is always easier to see beauty and kindness in others. But try taking a step back and imagine you are outside of your body looking at yourself from above, what do you see?

I have a little task for you, should you choose to take on a challenge! For 7 days I want you to write down 5 things each day that you love about yourself.

I have been doing this and it gives me such an amazing feeling, things come up I didn't even realise I loved about myself. I would love your feedback on this!

Love is the best medicine. Be kind to yourself, first and foremost. After all we need to take care of ourselves to then be the best we can for loving others.

A great example of this is when you go on holiday and once you are on the aircraft the flight attendant gives you a briefing on making sure you attend to your own oxygen mask before you help others. It makes much more sense to stabilise yourself, so you can be in much better service to help others.

When we fill up our own cup, we will be the very best version of ourselves and this will naturally lead us towards serving others from a loving place.

You are no good to others in your worst form.

People will see the best you and gravitate towards you. Do not be afraid to let your light shine brightly for others to see. They will also know how to treat you in the nicest way, as you have shown them how you want to be treated by loving yourself.

We don't have any control over what we think, but we can choose whether to give power to our thinking. Thoughts are just designed to pass on through us.
So, if we were to forget something or do something wrong then we are not to blame so why wouldn't we forgive ourselves? We innocently do the best we can, in any given moment, with the thinking we have.

That's all there is to it.

So, go on, off you go and get loving yourself! Trust me it's an amazing feeling...

"The more you love & value yourself, the easier it is for others to love & value you"

Anita Moorjani

Lucy Sheffield

Chapter 6 – Letting Go for a Peaceful Feeling

Oh, wow chapter 6 already, I really hope you are having some fun and learning lots...

There is so much to this understanding we really could go on all night, but I'll try not to waffle too much and keep you interested with my short chapters!

So...... letting go. What does this mean for you? Letting people off the hook for doing bad/wrong things? (Just as a reminder there are no bad/wrong things, only your view in that moment) Or forgiving people for their innocent thinking which YOU innocently felt upset by?

Remember people are always doing the best they can with the thinking they have got. We can't really ask for more from them. After all we are doing the same!

For me personally it makes my life easier if I let go of things. Or another way I prefer to see this is understanding my thinking.

When we insightfully see things as thought in the moment, there is no letting go that we have to do, it's done for us. It lets go of us, because we have erased its power. I feel kind and peaceful inside, and from experience I would much prefer to have this feeling than a horrible one.

It looks very much like we are letting people off from the things they are supposedly doing to us, but we are not, it is only another illusion in this game of life. All we are actually doing is freeing ourselves, creating peace instead of anger or resentment. We really are giving ourselves the peace of mind we deserve when we show compassion to others and forgive them.

Holding onto anger is like drinking poison and expecting the other person to die. It makes no sense. Forgiveness is so much more beneficial to our own peace of mind.

Let me ask you this... do you like the feeling of anger/upset/madness with someone or would it be nicer if you felt calm, compassion and love for the innocence they are showing?

It's all about being an example to people, helping them learn. Compassion comes naturally when we can see the other person is only guilty of believing their thinking in that moment. We can relate to this on a personal level, from this space the only thing to follow would be forgiveness.

Lucy Sheffield

"Be an example, show kindness to unkind people, and forgive people who don't deserve it, love unconditionally. YOUR actions always reflect who YOU are"

Unknown

I love to show up in the world as me, we only see the world as WE are, where we are at in our own mind. If I'm being kind, compassionate and loving to another, it's ONLY a reflection of me, nothing to do with them. It makes no difference if they are being angry or defensive, I will always be reflecting what I am feeling in the moment and nothing else. We are all the same. It's how we operate as humans.

Often people say to me "yeah but I can't just let them get away with it" or "it's not right, they shouldn't behave like that" etc., you get the idea. Well sure, if that's what you think then of course it's going to look like that for you.

But when you suddenly remember "oh hang on a minute this is what I am thinking right now, but does that mean I am always going to think that way?" NO of course not because thought is transparent, its energy, it moves, constantly, creating new things in different forms. The only way you can have a new experience, idea etc. is with a change of thought. Your mind needs to take a shift.

It's that simple!

I hear you saying, "Well how do I change my mind then?" or "I want a technique!"

I prefer to show you how things actually work, by explaining how we create our experience, then the simplest of things happens when we begin to see this on a deep level and our world opens up.

If I gave you techniques, you see, then all you are doing is copying what might work for me. The technique won't necessarily work the same for you or anyone else. When we learn about how our experiences are created, then you can create your own "techniques" (if that's what works for you) – following your own wisdom in each moment.

The best wisdom I have found is to keep bringing it back to understanding where your experience is being created from, in that moment, that's the simplicity of it. Personally, I find that easier than having to go meditate or anything else. But that's just me!

Mostly though it is even simpler than that. By understanding that we think, and that our thoughts are only passing through, those thoughts begin to change all by themselves. We don't need to know what the thinking means, or any of that, or why we think what we do. All those things are just adding more thought. What helps us is in any situation is having a clear mind and space for new thought. Less on our minds is always the key. It's like magic really.

Lucy Sheffield

Chapter 7 – We are all the same!

Now let's see who is going to argue here with me about this? Is it true? "How can we all be the same?" I hear you protest! Some people are naturally horrible, always angry, and always nasty to others. And some people are always kind and get walked all over etc. etc.

Trust me I've been there, I can see how it can look that way. Since coming across these life changing principles back in 2011, I now see most of us are seeing things backwards. Let me explain what I mean here (or at least try).

For years I thought life was "out there" and things were happening to me. People did horrible things and used me, and why did I deserve that? I wasn't a bad person particularly. I tried to be nice and please people all the time.

Lucy Sheffield

I was shy, scared of everything and everyone, and most certainly did not love or value myself. It looked very much to me like I had to have things to feel ok; money, possessions, love etc. I'm sure you get the picture.

It looked like these things were going to make me feel happy and secure. So why was I not getting them? Why did I have a job where I didn't earn much money? Why did I always drink alcohol to give me more confidence which led to people liking me better? Why couldn't I find someone who loved me for who I was? The questions were endless....

I began to see that, but for our thinking in the moment, we are all the same, created from the same huge ball of universal energy, moulded into different forms. Like a child creates shapes from a ball of plasticine.

"All we are is peace, love and wisdom with the power to create the illusion that we are not"

Jack Pransky

Understanding this had such an enormous impact on my life, but quite slowly at first. I started to just generally feel calmer; it felt like "hang on a minute if I am love at my core what the hell is there to fear?"

And the more deeply I saw this the more confident I got, the more thinking dropped away the more love shone through me. The more of me I could give to others, freely. I wasn't scared any more. I didn't need money, a good job, a girlfriend to be happy. I was happiness, joy, peace, love, god (any word that fits for you).

It was my birth right.

We are all born with it, but we lose it the moment we start to believe every thought we have. Or we take on other peoples beliefs as if they are truths.

I love the analogy of being like the sky... At our deepest core we are the sky, which is our true essence, it cannot be taken away from us. Yes, it can become clouded over with all sorts of weather (i.e. thoughts) we can have cloudy days, rainy days, foggy days etc. etc... And this makes the sky look different, but it never changes the fact that the sky still stays there unharmed, untouched, perfect whole, complete and pure. This is our true spiritual nature, just sitting there unharmed, just beneath the human thought storms. Strong & firm, a foundation for us to build on and create our experiences in human form.

Ooooooh this got a bit deep didn't it! Hope you're keeping up!!

So, the only thing that separates us from any other human is our thinking.
We are all the same underneath at our true core, and then it can begin to look to us like some people are horrid and some are kind because of the thinking we are believing.

When we don't know that it's thought causing it, we easily get carried along with the angry thoughts and act form them. When we see and understand them for what they are, we are more likely to rethink (naturally) before reacting from that angry/hurtful place, and connect back to our true selves (love).

My wonderful Auntie Deb (who introduced me to the principles) talks a lot about people pleasing, people squashing or being in service. I'll do my best to describe this in the way she does...

Imagine a line drawn on paper and at one end there is people pleasing, the other end is people squashing and the middle is being in service. The way I see it is a lot of the time many of us are either people pleasing (this to me means doing things for others because you want them to like you) or people squashing (this to me means manipulating people to do what you want).

Both of these things look like they come from a fear of losing someone. If we are nice to people and they then like you it feels safe, and equally if you cleverly manipulate someone to do what you want them to do, you are in control of them, so you think they can't leave you.

However, here comes the best bit, if you are in the middle of these 2 places then it's what Deb describes as, being in service. This naturally comes when we are feeling truly connected, whole and complete, lacking in nothing, really really deeply seeing and knowing we don't **NEED** anything from outside of us to be happy or ok. From this space we are genuinely being our true selves and giving anything from there can only be the best for everyone involved. This is being in service to the world. We can only be giving the best. I really hope this is making some kind of sense, all I can say is I am thoroughly enjoying writing it.

Special thanks to Debra for letting me use her ideas in this chapter!

Lucy Sheffield

So just to sum up; we have it the wrong way around – we don't need anything in the outside world to be different for us to be ok, because it's all created from inside. We always have everything we need, and we are all the same, fundamentally at our spiritual core...We are all the sky.... You get me?

The Table with No Edge

Chapter 8 - Fun

Good morning! Hope you are well today my lovely reader and new friend.

I would love to talk in this chapter about living life and having fun. I would probably say I've always tried to have lots of fun in my life and always been the life and soul of the party.

However, since coming across the principles this has been one of the things I notice in my life that I do even more of now. I spend as much time as I can having lots of fun and doing all the things that I enjoy - being around all the people I love and who bring out the best in me. When we can be our true selves, we have less on our minds and this allows us creative space.

I feel like Peter Pan, I've never really grown up. I spend a hell of a lot of time being silly, having fun, laughing and not taking anything seriously. It's even scientifically proven (I think) that laughter is one of the best medicines.

Laughing causes the release of endorphins (that's the most scientific I'm going to get!) – the happiness chemical!

Life looks more like a game to me, to be lived, enjoyed, and to have fun... there is so much to explore and so much fun to have, but we tend to miss so much of it because we think we have to do certain things. For example, house work, making a living. All the boring everyday things that we have made up that we have to do. I bet you have a list of jobs and never want to do any of them, or at least a lot of the time you don't want to do them. Why do we put ourselves through this? We have made up that we need to do this stuff and then we moan and don't want to do it.

It is more beneficial to the world, and everyone in it, if we are spending time having fun and doing the things that bring out the best in us, following our passions.

One of my favourite sayings I've come across in the principles is...

"do more of what you love"

The more I find myself doing fun things, the more it frees me up and I then feel ok to do my "to do" lists some of the time as well. It all gets done exactly when it is meant to.

When we relax, we trust in the system behind life. It's all being done for us, we just have to sit back, relax and enjoy the ride, literally! So, what is left for us to actually do then? Well this is how I see it – sod all! That's right, sod all, so what does that leave then – plenty of time for enjoying life and having lots and lots of fun.

The system behind life (the 3 principles) is running the show. It's how our life is set up. Very much like a roller coaster at a fun fair (very relevant to this chapter called fun!)

Life is the same, we are here for the ride, to relax, enjoy, take the ups with the downs, and just go with the flow.

One of my favourite sayings, that has stuck with me for a few years, was something I heard Michael Neill say in one of his speeches, at the annual 3 principle London Tikun conference. It went something like this – "imagine you are at a theme park or similar and you can have the choice of taking a tour around. You can pay a small fee and just see some of it or pay a little more and you get the full experience". (This might not be exactly how he worded it so don't quote me on it).

He goes on to say wouldn't you want the full experience? He then likens it to life, as humans we are getting the full experience which includes the good, the bad and the ugly. Sure, sometimes things come up in life that really aren't too nice, but imagine if we didn't get to experience it all. How dull would it be, just getting the good bits or the bad bits?

Well the way he explained it was amazing, and I am totally in agreement that I want the full tour. I've signed on the dotted line, and I'm sure enjoying the ride so far!

I just saw this awesome quote and it seems very fitting for what I have been trying to portray in this chapter, so I thought I would share it with you...

"Life is a roller coaster, you can either scream every time you hit a bump, or you can throw your hands up in the air and enjoy it"

Unknown

Lucy Sheffield

So, to sum up – go out have some fun, relax and enjoy your life. I'm not sure what happens upon death, but I reckon we only get one life as we know it, so do what you love! From this genuine place all the other stuff that looks important - money, bills etc. etc. - will fall into place, it just does!

The Table with No Edge

Chapter 9 – Life is an Illusion

As we are nearing the end of this book I would like to just explore this mind-blowing topic with you.

As we discussed in chapter 7 - we are all the same underneath. We are all created from the same spiritual essence, the truth, formed into different energy in the moment. This, to me, looks like there is something larger than us humans in control of the bigger picture (aka life as we know it in our human form).

I'm not sure, with our human minds, we can comprehend the hugeness of this most of the time – it's not for us to know right now in human form. Who knows what we may discover when our human form ends, and we are back into oneness.

If we are creating our experience moment to moment through the gift of thought, which is constantly changing then it looks very clear to me that all we are ever experiencing is an illusion.

"Reality is merely an illusion, albeit a very persistent one."

Albert Einstein

Things look a certain way for an amount of time, then they change again. Truth never changes, it's a constant. We know that we are always going to feel what we think. That will not change.

Illusion is always changing because it is a perspective, and as we know our perception is always changing as we believe and see things differently, as we move through life.

Things are never what they appear to be. If we go back to the straw in the water, as in chapter 1, we see things as we are, not as they are. We see an illusion before our very eyes, created through us from a much larger power, and seeing this deeply & insightfully is truly mind blowing & life changing!

Everything we are seeing and believing is simply not truth. Its disguised very cleverly to look like truth, but it's all created within the illusion we know us as this world.

So, if it's all an illusion as I am suggesting, then can you see how anything in physical form does not really exist, only via our thought in the moment...

The Table with No Edge

It's a funny one to grasp because we are very brought into physical things being there as they are solid. I mean we can see things, they are there in front of us, of course they are real.

It looks the same to me when we truly believe something to be true in our minds, it looks fixed and solid as does the table. The more we are open to things perhaps not being fixed and definitely what we believe them to be the more we can begin to see things in a different way.

A by-product of this is we begin to see where we have limited ourselves and we begin to see we have unlimited potential as human beings.

If the table was edgeless and never ended it would expand and connect to everything and everyone.... we are all connected in this way as humans too.

When we feel connected to that higher source, that universal energy, we expand and become limitless as the illusion of fear drops away. Once fear has dropped away then all we are left with is unconditional love. And when we aren't attached to conditions, to anything having to be a certain way in order for us to feel ok, then we are in our highest place of service to ourselves, which subsequently is the best for everyone else.

From this place we can create the most wonderful things out in the world because it is effortless to us in this state. We are simply doing things for the love of them.
Any other reason has dropped away. This is the freedom we are all seeking as a race – to be who we truly are – freely without worry for what others think, shining our light brightly for ourselves and others.
An implication of this is that other people are naturally drawn and attracted to us, they want a bit of this, and so it rubs off, like a ripple effect, spreading world wide – The Peace, Love and Wisdom that we already are, changing the world as we know it, one thought at a time.

The Table with No Edge

If the table has an edge then it is limited, it ends. If it doesn't then its open to being unlimited, the same as us in human form, we are unlimited, but we limit ourselves and can't see that we do. If we are edgeless like the table then we expand and connect, and wonderful things can be created as we open up to more possibilities, they become visible to us. Our world opens up to opportunities we never before saw as possible.

Lucy Sheffield

"Every man takes the limits of his own field of vision for the limits of the world"

Arthur Schopenhauer

The Table with No Edge

So, does the table have an edge or is it not really there at all? Is it all part of the illusion too?

I will leave you to think about that one for yourself.... who knows what could come up for you.

Lucy Sheffield

Chapter 10 – Bye Bye for Now

Just a small closing chapter for you to sum up a little.
I've thoroughly enjoyed writing and creating this book. I really hope you have all loved it as much as I have in doing it.

It can sometimes be very difficult to describe the truth to which these amazing principles are pointing to. It's trying to explain about something that isn't in form, it isn't tangible, we can't see it and we only have words to describe it, which can mean so many different things to each of us.

However, what we can remember is to look for the feeling. Always follow the feeling you have in your heart that will be connecting you to the highest wisdom of this universe. I can promise you. You won't go far wrong.

Love is always the answer - it never matters what the question is.

Bye bye for now friends... watch this space!

Lucy Sheffield

Look out for our other books available on Amazon...

Dare2BU (By Debra Simmons)

And coming soon....

Inside Out Uni-Verse

You can follow Lucy and find out more of what her and the Dare2BU team are up to, and how you contact us via our website
www.debrasimmons.co.uk

Lucy Sheffield

About the Author

For most of her 30 something years Lucy struggled with being at peace with herself. Whilst talking with her aunty Deb about 'something I didn't understand but liked to hear more of' Lucy had some deep insights. These insights pointed Lucy back to her own innate health and resilience.

She is now someone who is so comfortable being herself it is difficult to imagine this ever not being the case.

Lucy has spent the last 6 years seeking out people who share the same understanding of innate health and resilience as she does in order to deepen her own, and others, clarity.

Lucy recently graduated from the "Debra Simmons Mentoring Programme" and has recently moved to Devon to follow her passion to share the principles with the ongoing support of Deb.

She runs weekly meet-up groups, locally, in Devon and works alongside Deb, her good friend Ju, and her sister Bec, running workshops, retreats and conferences pointing people back to their natural well-being.

To see more of what Lucy is up to visit www.Debrasimmons.co.uk

Lucy Sheffield

The Table with No Edge

Lucy Sheffield

The Table with No Edge

Printed in Poland
by Amazon Fulfillment
Poland Sp. z o.o., Wrocław